What are cumulus clouds?

Lynn Peppas

Clouds Close-Up

Author
Lynn Peppas

Publishing plan research and development
Sean Charlebois, Reagan Miller
Crabtree Publishing Company

Editorial director
Kathy Middleton

Editor
Reagan Miller

Proofreader
Crystal Sikkens

Photo research
Allison Napier, Samara Parent

Design
Samara Parent

**Production coordinator
and prepress technician**
Samara Parent

Print coordinator
Katherine Berti

Illustrations
Barbara Bedell: pages 6–7 (except water droplets)
Katherine Bert: page 7 (water droplets)

Photographs
istockphoto.com: pages 11 (middle)
Shutterstock.com: title page, contents page, pages 8 (all), 11 (top), 12,
    15 (bottom), 16, 18 (all), 21 (top), 22 (left, middle, bottom)
Thinkstock.com: pages 5, 10, 13, 15 (top), 17, 19, 21 (bottom), 22 (top right)
Wikimedia commons: ©Simon Eugste: page 14; ©Nicholas: pages 11 (bottom), 20

Library and Archives Canada Cataloguing in Publication

Peppas, Lynn
    What are cumulus clouds? / Lynn Peppas.

(Clouds close-up)
Includes index.
Issued also in electronic format.
ISBN 978-0-7787-4474-0 (bound).--ISBN 978-0-7787-4479-5 (pbk.)

    1. Cumulus--Juvenile literature. 2. Weather--Juvenile literature.
I. Title. II. Series: Peppas, Lynn. Clouds close-up.

QC921.43.C8P47 2012   j551.57'6   C2012-901512-1

Library of Congress Cataloging-in-Publication Data

CIP available at Library of Congress

Crabtree Publishing Company
www.crabtreebooks.com   1-800-387-7650

Printed in Canada/042012/KR20120316

Published in Canada
Crabtree Publishing
616 Welland Ave.
St. Catharines, Ontario
L2M 5V6

Published in the United States
Crabtree Publishing
PMB 59051
350 Fifth Avenue, 59th Floor
New York, New York 10118

Published in the United Kingdom
Crabtree Publishing
Maritime House
Basin Road North, Hove
BN41 1WR

Published in Australia
Crabtree Publishing
3 Charles Street
Coburg North
VIC 3058

Contents

Send in the clouds

Watching clouds in the sky is like watching a magic show! Clouds change shape and some even disappear right before your eyes! Where do clouds come from and where do they go? Keep reading to find out!

4

Three main kinds of clouds

Clouds are made up of water droplets or ice crystals. Each droplet is so small that it floats in the air. Clouds have different shapes, sizes, and colors. Different kinds of clouds bring different kinds of **weather**. Clouds give clues as to what the weather will be like.

The water cycle

The **water cycle** describes the movement of water on, in, and above the earth. Clouds are an important part of this cycle. Follow the arrows below to learn more about water's amazing journey!

*Water vapor floats up into the air. The air is colder higher up. The water vapor cools and **condenses**, or changes into water droplets. Millions of water droplets join together to form a cloud.*

The Sun heats the water in oceans, lakes, rivers, and even puddles!

*The Sun's heat makes some of the water **evaporate**, or change into **water vapor**.*

water droplets

The water droplets fall from clouds as rain, snow, or another form of **precipitation**.

Cloud names

stratus clouds

The word stratus means "layer."

cumulus clouds

The word cumulus means "heap" or "pile."

More than 200 years ago, a man named Luke Howard gave names to different kinds of clouds. He named the clouds using **Latin** words that describe the cloud's shape.

cirrus clouds

The word cirrus means "curls of hair."

The three main kinds of clouds are **cirrus**, **stratus**, and **cumulus** clouds.

Look at the pictures above to learn what each cloud name means.

How high in the sky?

Some clouds form high in the sky. Other kinds of clouds form so low they touch the ground. There are three words used to describe how high clouds form in the sky. They are strato, alto, and cirro.

Cloud levels

High clouds

Cloud names that begin with "cirro" are the highest clouds in the sky.

Middle clouds

Clouds in the middle of the sky have names that start with "alto."

Low clouds

Clouds that form low in the sky have "strato" in their names.

cirrocumulus clouds

altocumulus clouds

stratocumulus clouds

What are cumulus clouds?

Cumulus clouds are sometimes called "fair-weather clouds." When you see them the weather is usually nice and sunny.

Cumulus clouds are bright white clouds with puffy tops and flat bottoms. They look like floating piles of cotton balls. The weather is usually sunny when you see them in the sky.

How cumulus clouds form

Cumulus clouds are made up of tiny water droplets.
Most form at around 1 mile (2 kilometers) from
Earth's surface. At this height the air is usually
warm enough to let the cloud gather more and
more droplets through the water cycle.

Stormy weather

If you see cumulus clouds growing taller and darker, beware! This is a sign that a storm is on its way! The cumulus cloud may be changing into a cumulonimbus cloud. Nimbus is a Latin word that means "rain." The word nimbus or nimbo is added to the name of a cloud that brings rain, snow, or other forms of precipitation.

Cumulonimbus clouds

Cumulonimbus clouds are the only clouds that make hail.

Thunderstorms come from cumulonimbus clouds. In fact, these clouds are also known as "thunderheads" because they bring heavy rain, thunder, lightning, and even **hail**. Hail is small balls of ice that fall from cumulonimbus clouds. One ball of hail is called a hailstone.

hail

Clouds on the move

Cumulus clouds move and change. All clouds are moved by **wind**. Wind is moving air. Sometimes strong winds push cumulus clouds higher in the sky. These clouds are called altocumulus clouds.

Altocumulus clouds

Altocumulus clouds are usually light gray. They form in bunches. Some people think a bunch of altocumulus clouds look like a flock, or group, of sheep in the sky. Altocumulus clouds can be a sign that rainy weather is on its way.

Cirrocumulus clouds

A sky with cirrocumulus clouds is sometimes called a "mackerel sky." This is because some people think the cloud's ripple pattern looks like the scales on a fish.

scales on a mackerel fish

Cirrocumulus clouds are the highest-forming cumulus clouds in the sky. The air at this height is very cold. Because of this, cirrocumulus clouds are made up of ice crystals. Cirrocumulus clouds form in ripples or small waves.

Cirrocumulus weather

Small patches of cirrocumulus clouds are a sign of sunny weather. A large cirrocumulus cloud that covers the sky may mean rain is coming later in the day.

Look at the cirrocumulus clouds in the picture above. What kind of weather do you think they will bring?

Stratocumulus clouds

altocumulus

stratocumulus

Cumulus clouds that form low in the sky are called stratocumulus clouds. Stratocumulus clouds are lumpy and gray. They sometimes form in rows.

Stratocumulus weather

Stratocumulus clouds may bring light rain that is called **drizzle**. These clouds usually mean that stormy weather is either coming soon, or just leaving.

Stratocumulus clouds have patches of blue sky between them.

Make your own hail!

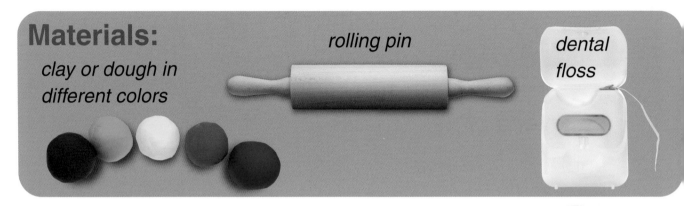

Materials:

clay or dough in different colors

rolling pin

dental floss

Directions:

1. Take a piece of clay and roll it into a small ball, about the size of a gum ball.

2. Next, take the same amount of clay in a different color and flatten it using your rolling pin. Wrap the flat piece of clay around your clay ball.

3. Repeat step 2 to add layers of different colored clay to your ball. Try to make your clay ball the size of a golf ball.

4. Use a piece of dental floss to split your clay ball down the center. Your ball of clay has many different layers. This is how a hailstone would look if you cut it in half!

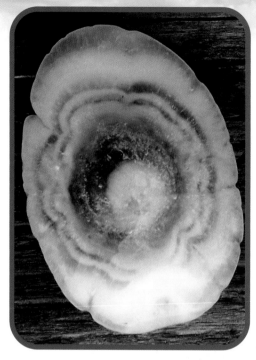

This hailstone has been cut in half. Can you see the layers of water and ice in it?

Explanation: Strong winds push water droplets up and down inside a cumulonimbus cloud. The droplets freeze at the top of the cloud where it is cold and begin to melt at the bottom of the cloud where it is warmer. This movement causes layers of water and ice to form around the droplet. The frozen droplet then falls from the cloud as hail.

Words to know

cirrus Thin, high-forming clouds made of ice crystals

condense To change from a gas to a liquid

cumulus Puffy, white clouds

drizzle A light, misty rain

evaporate To change from a liquid to a gas

hail Frozen balls of ice that fall from clouds

Latin An old language that was used thousands of years ago

precipitation Rain, snow, or hail that falls from clouds to the earth

stratus Thick, gray, low-forming clouds

water cycle Describes how water moves between Earth's surface and the sky

water vapor Water that has changed from a liquid to a gas

weather What the air is like at a certain time and place

wind Naturally moving air

Index

Learning more

Books:

What is Climate? by Bobbie Kalman. Crabtree Publishing Company, 2012.

Changing Weather: Storms by Bobbie Kalman. Crabtree Publishing Company, 2006.

The Weather by Deborah Chancellor. Crabtree Publishing Company, 2010.

Websites:

http://eo.ucar.edu/webweather/cloudhome.html

www.weatherwizkids.com

www.northcanton.sparcc.org/~elem/interactivities/clouds/cloudsread.html